FOR ORGANS, PIANOS & ELECTRONIC KEYBOARDS

E-Z PLAY TODAY

96

MAMMA MIA!™

THE MOVIE SOUNDTRACK FEATURING THE SONGS OF ABBA®

ISBN 978-1-4234-8094-5

HAL•LEONARD®
CORPORATION
7777 W. BLUEMOUND RD. P.O. BOX 13819 MILWAUKEE, WI 53213

Visit Hal Leonard Online at
www.halleonard.com

Dancing Queen

Registration 2
Rhythm: Rock or 8 Beat

Words and Music by Benny Andersson,
Björn Ulvaeus and Stig Anderson

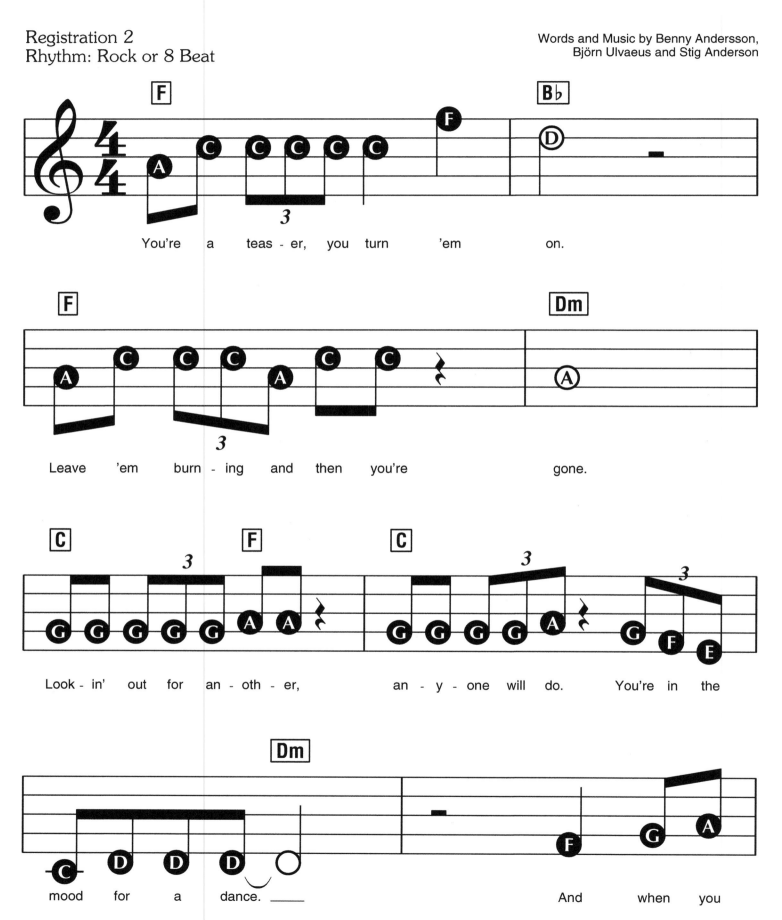

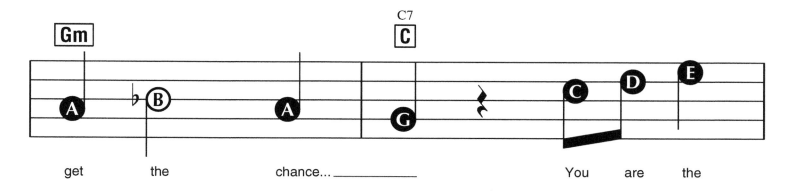

get the chance... _____ You are the

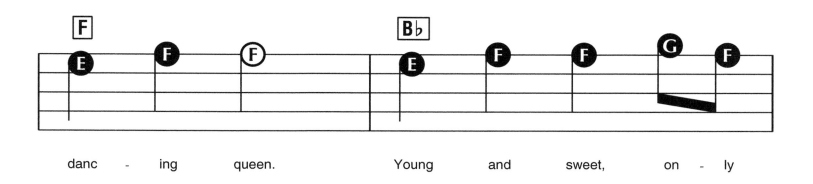

danc - ing queen. Young and sweet, on - ly

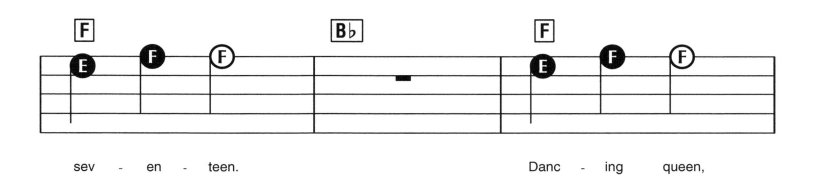

sev - en - teen. Danc - ing queen,

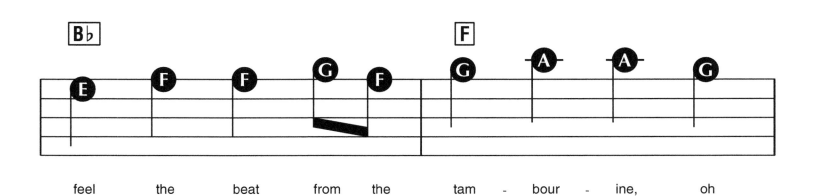

feel the beat from the tam - bour - ine, oh

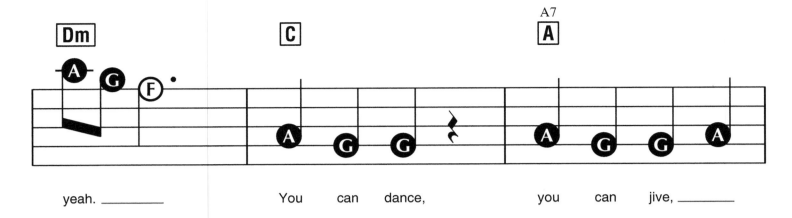

yeah. _____ You can dance, you can jive, _____

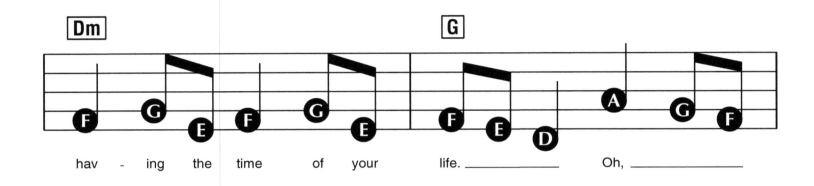

hav - ing the time of your life. _____ Oh, _____

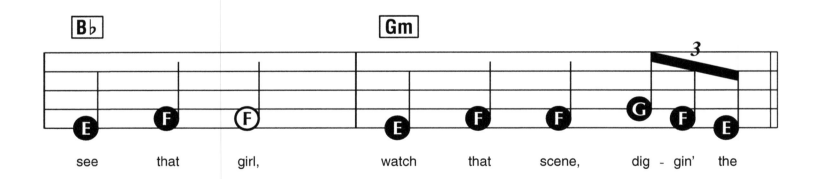

see that girl, watch that scene, dig - gin' the

Repeat and Fade

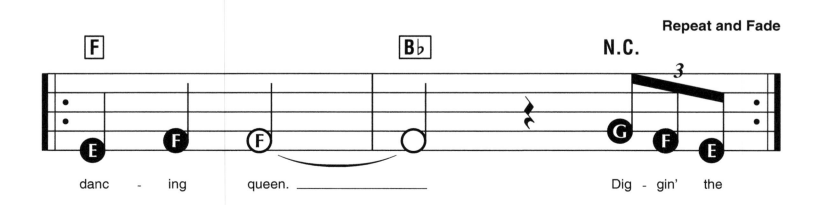

danc - ing queen. _____ Dig - gin' the

Honey, Honey

Registration 2
Rhythm: Dance or Rock

Words and Music by Benny Andersson,
Bjorn Ulvaeus and Stig Anderson

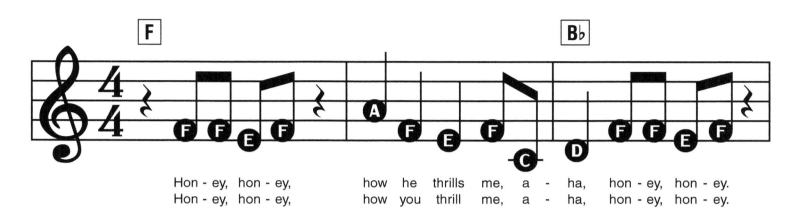

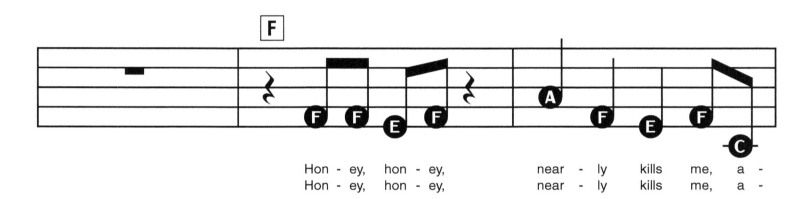

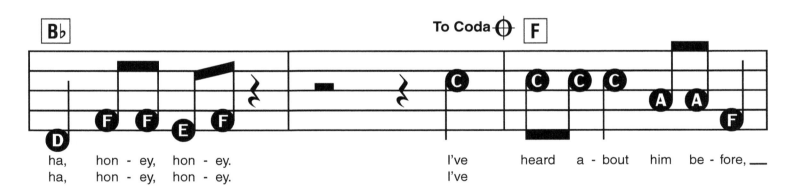

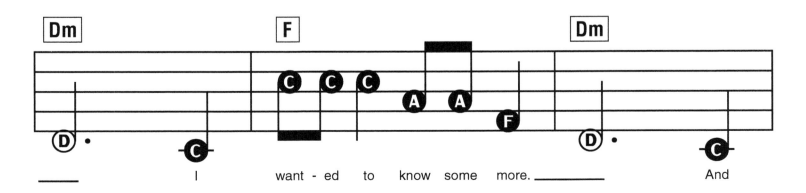

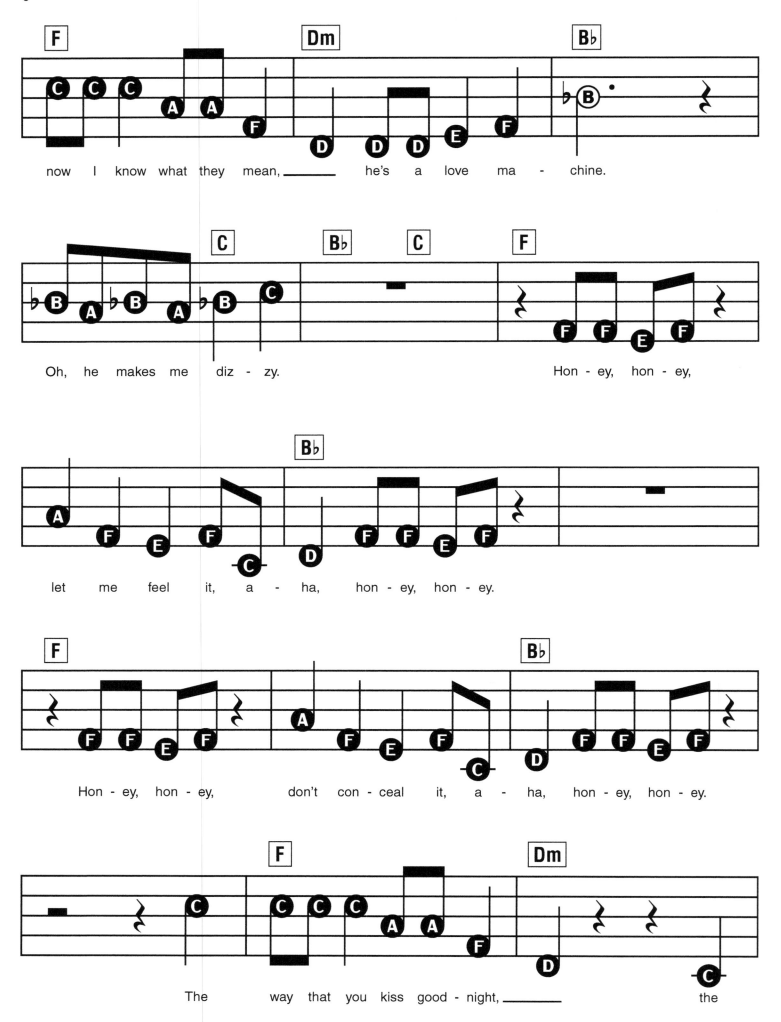

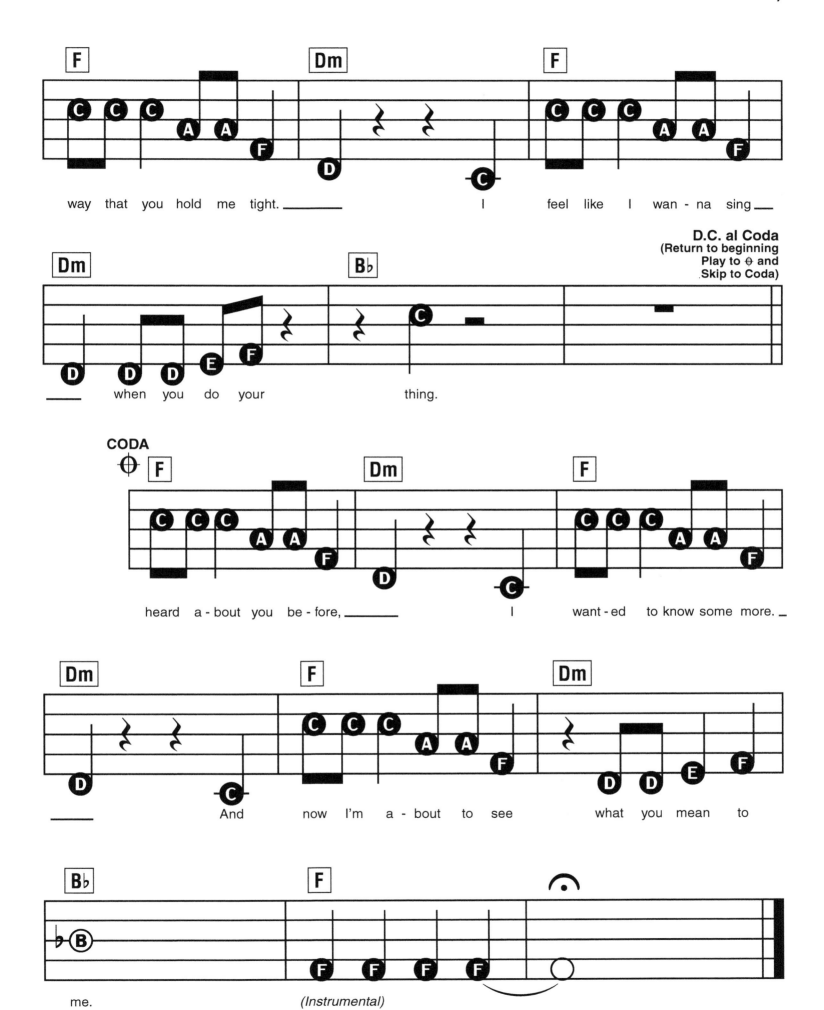

Does Your Mother Know

Registration 2
Rhythm: Rock

Words and Music by Benny Andersson
and Bjorn Ulvaeus

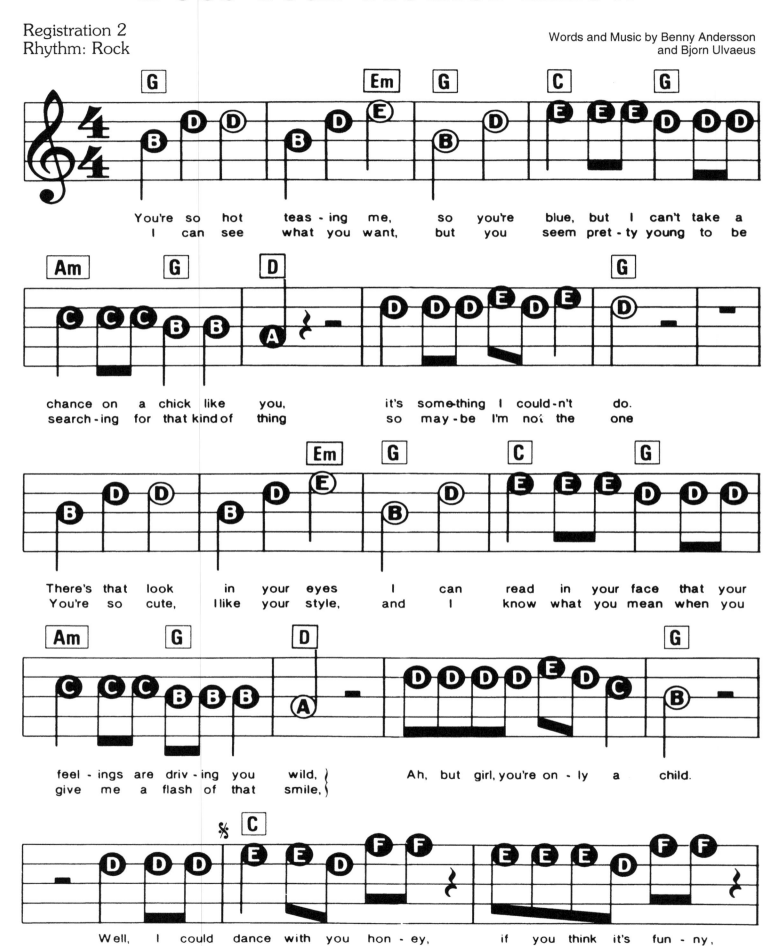

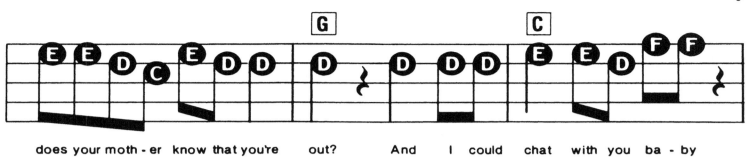

does your moth - er know that you're out? And I could chat with you ba - by

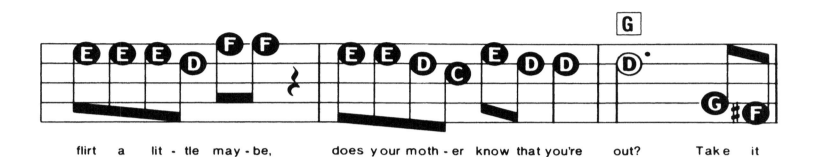

flirt a lit - tle may - be, does your moth - er know that you're out? Take it

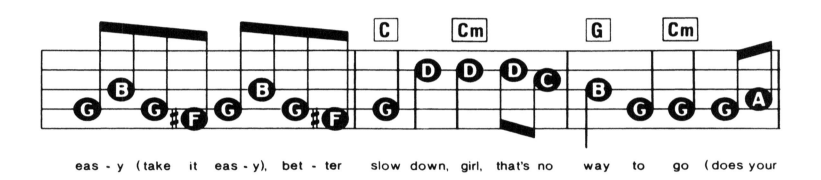

eas - y (take it eas - y), bet - ter slow down, girl, that's no way to go (does your

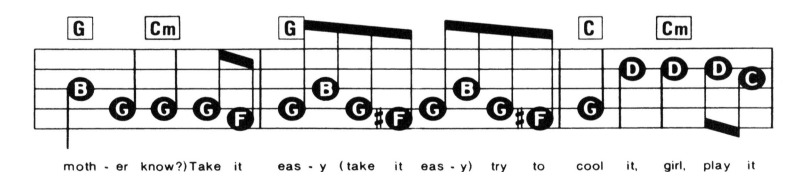

moth - er know?) Take it eas - y (take it eas - y) try to cool it, girl, play it

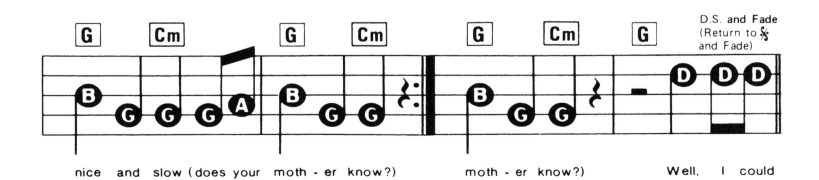

nice and slow (does your moth - er know?) moth - er know?) Well, I could

Gimme! Gimme! Gimme!
(A Man after Midnight)

Registration 4
Rhythm: Rock

Words and Music by Benny Andersson
and Bjorn Ulvaeus

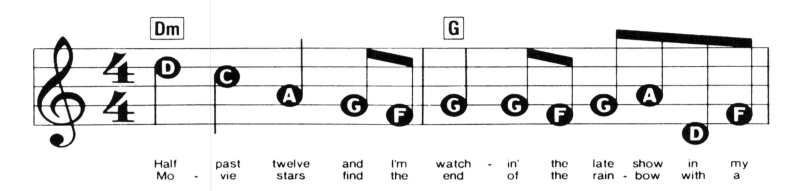

Half past twelve and I'm watch-in' the late show in my
Mo - vie stars find the end of the rain - bow with a

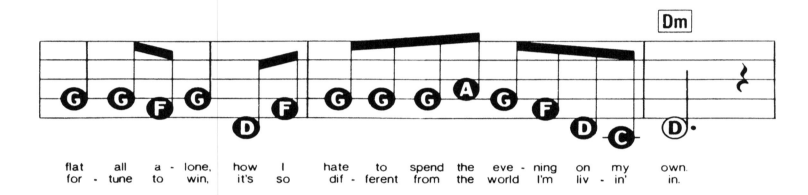

flat all a - lone, how I hate to spend the eve - ning on my own.
for - tune to win, it's so dif - ferent from the world I'm liv - in' in.

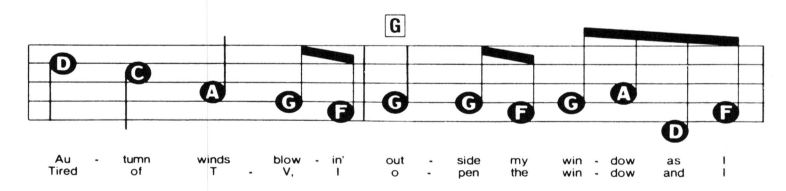

Au - tumn winds blow - in' out - side my win - dow as I
Tired of T.V., I o - pen the win - dow and I

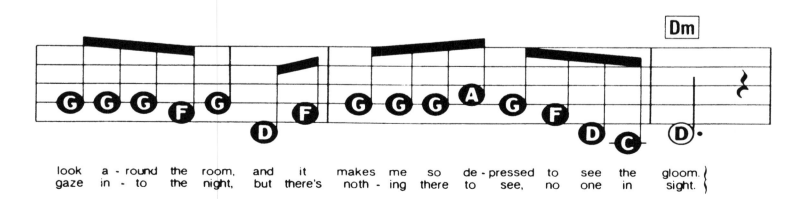

look a - round the room, and it makes me so de - pressed to see the gloom.
gaze in - to the night, but there's noth - ing there to see, no one in sight.

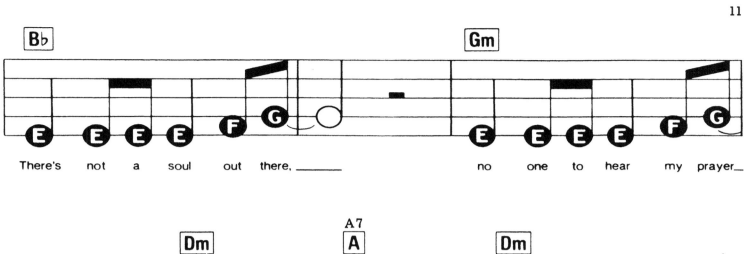

There's not a soul out there, _____ no one to hear my prayer__

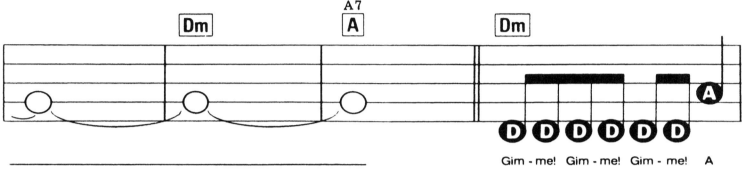

Gim - me! Gim - me! Gim - me! A

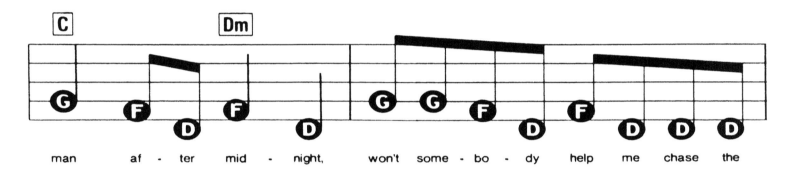

man af - ter mid - night, won't some - bo - dy help me chase the

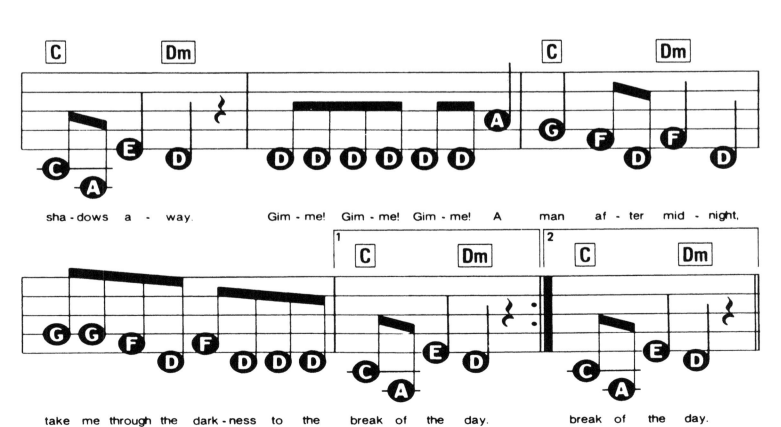

sha - dows a - way. Gim - me! Gim - me! Gim - me! A man af - ter mid - night,

take me through the dark - ness to the break of the day. break of the day.

I Have a Dream

Registration 3
Rhythm: Ballad

Words and Music by Benny Andersson
and Bjorn Ulvaeus

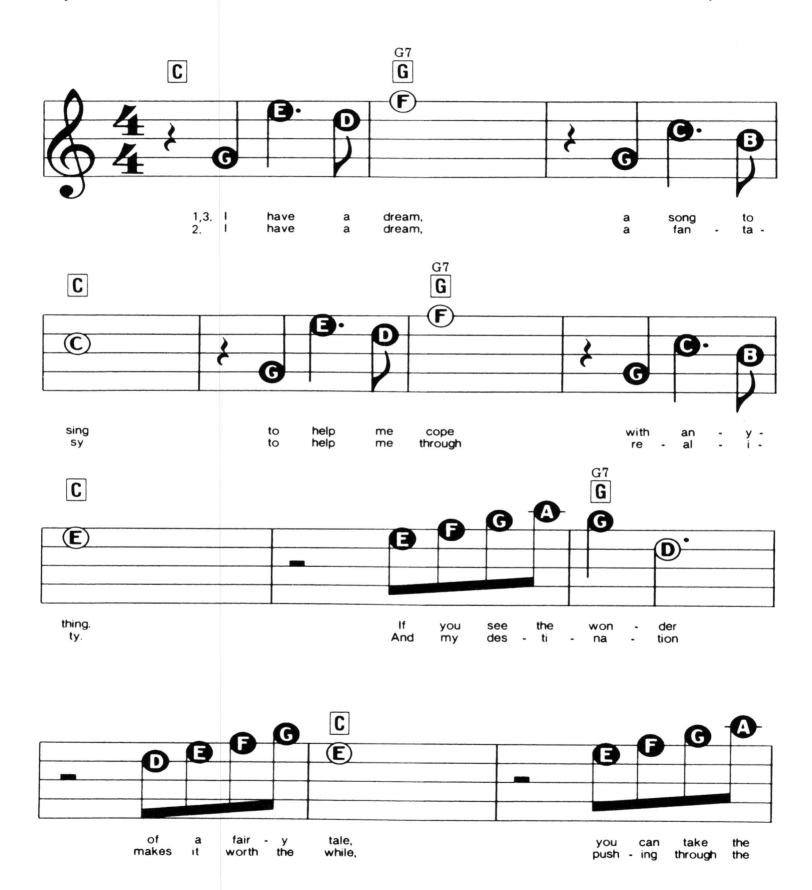

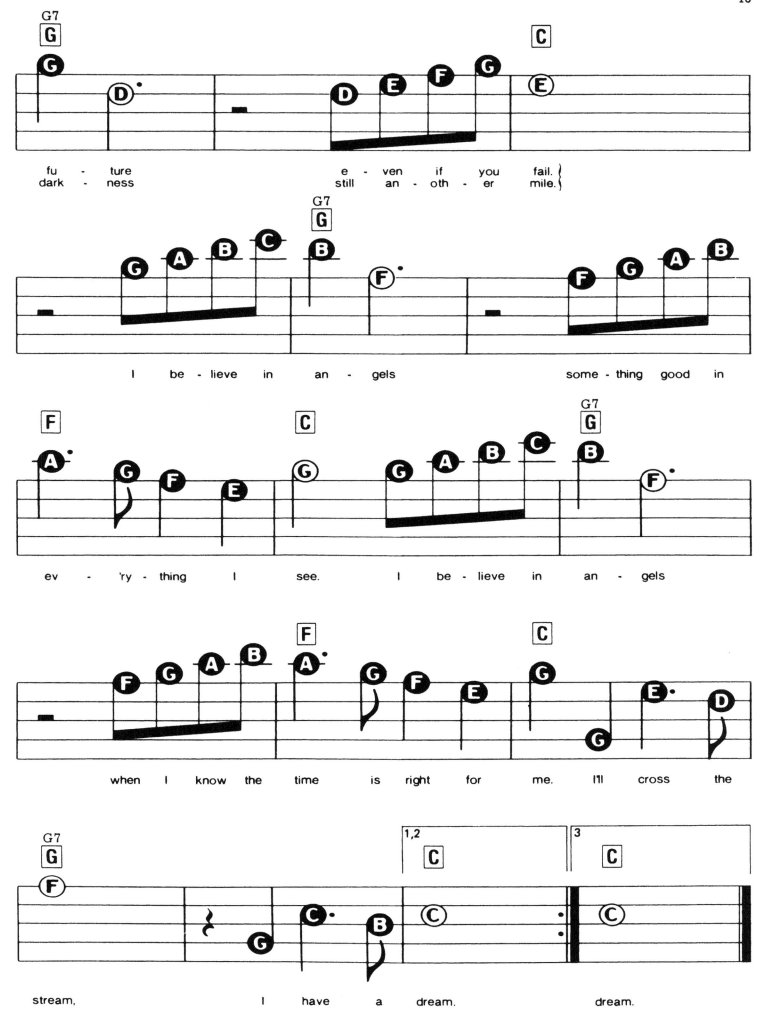

fu - ture   e - ven if you fail.
dark - ness   still an - oth - er mile.

I be - lieve in an - gels   some - thing good in

ev - 'ry - thing I see.   I be - lieve in an - gels

when I know the time is right for me. I'll cross the

stream,   I have a dream.   dream.

Lay All Your Love on Me

Registration 5
Rhythm: Disco or Rock

Words and Music by Benny Andersson
and Bjorn Ulvaeus

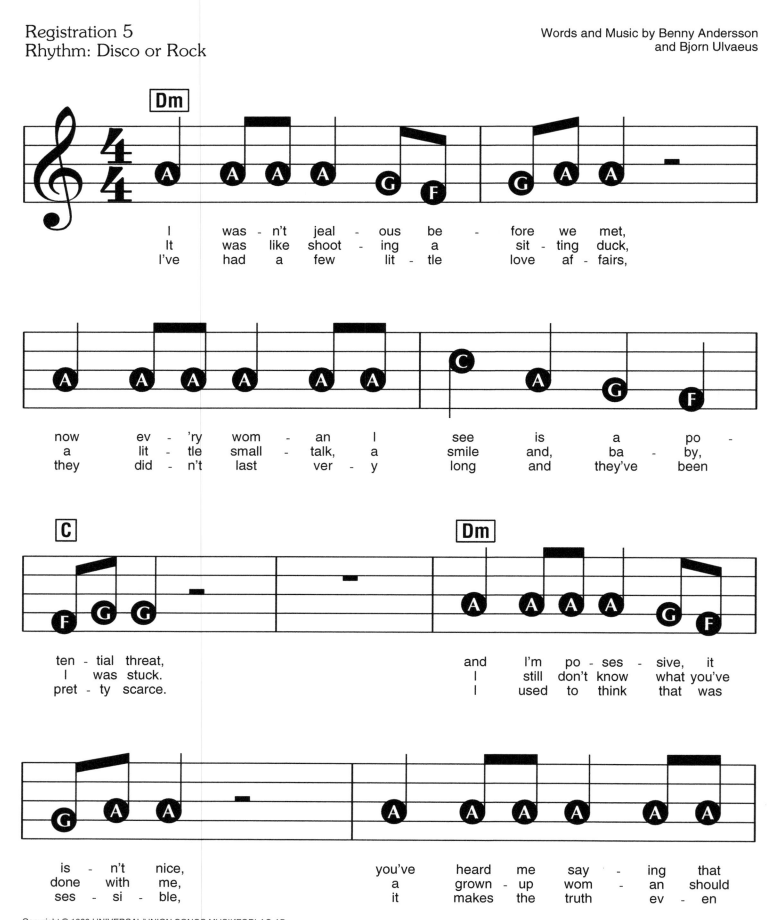

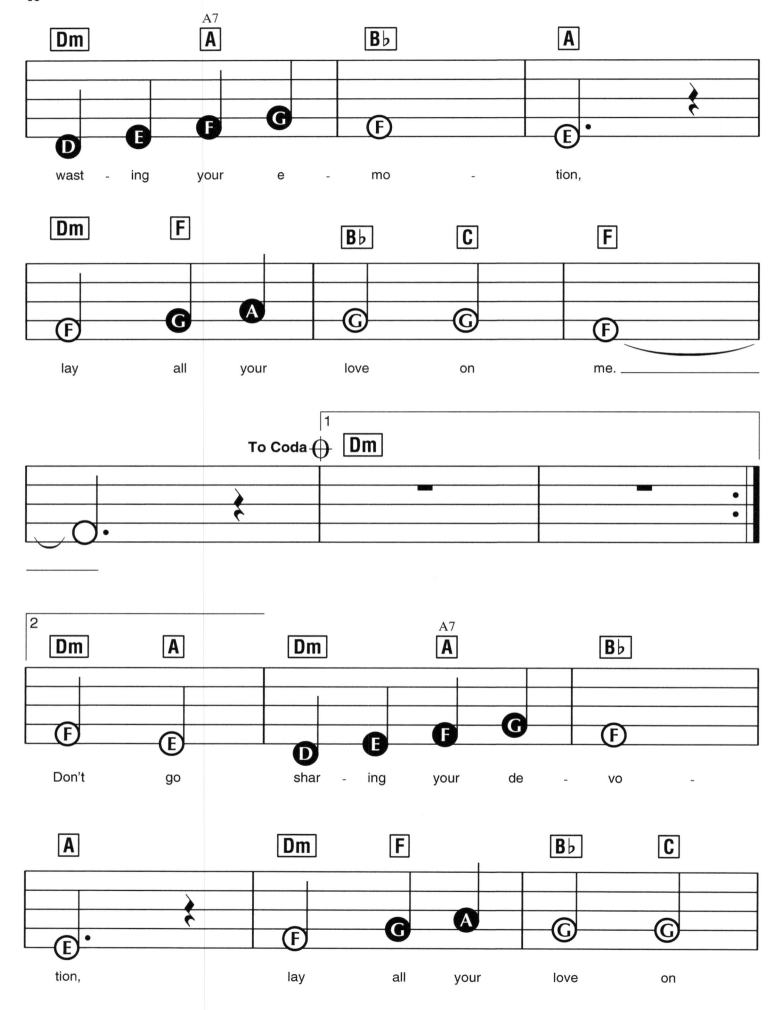

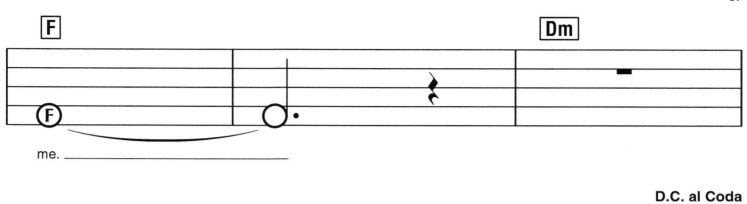

D.C. al Coda
(Go back to the beginning, play to
⊕ and skip to Coda)

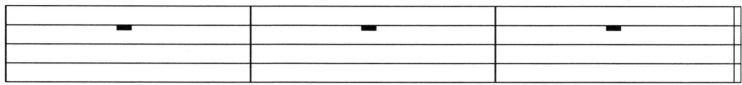

CODA

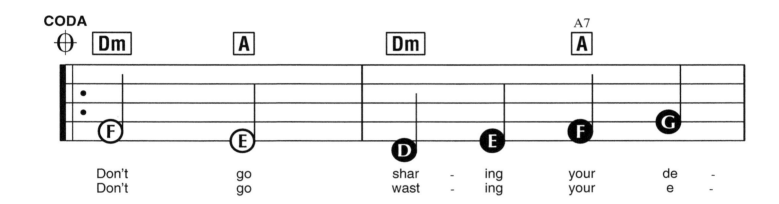

Don't   go   shar - ing your de -
Don't   go   wast - ing your e -

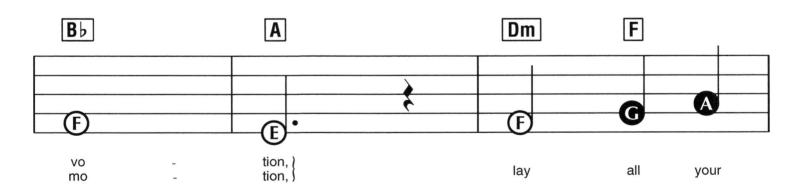

vo - tion,
mo - tion,   lay all your

Repeat and Fade

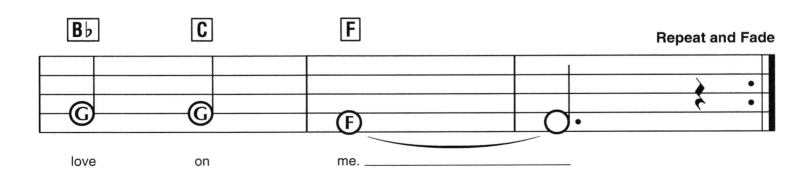

love   on   me.

Mamma Mia

Registration 3
Rhythm: Rock

Words and Music by Benny Andersson,
Björn Ulvaeus and Stig Anderson

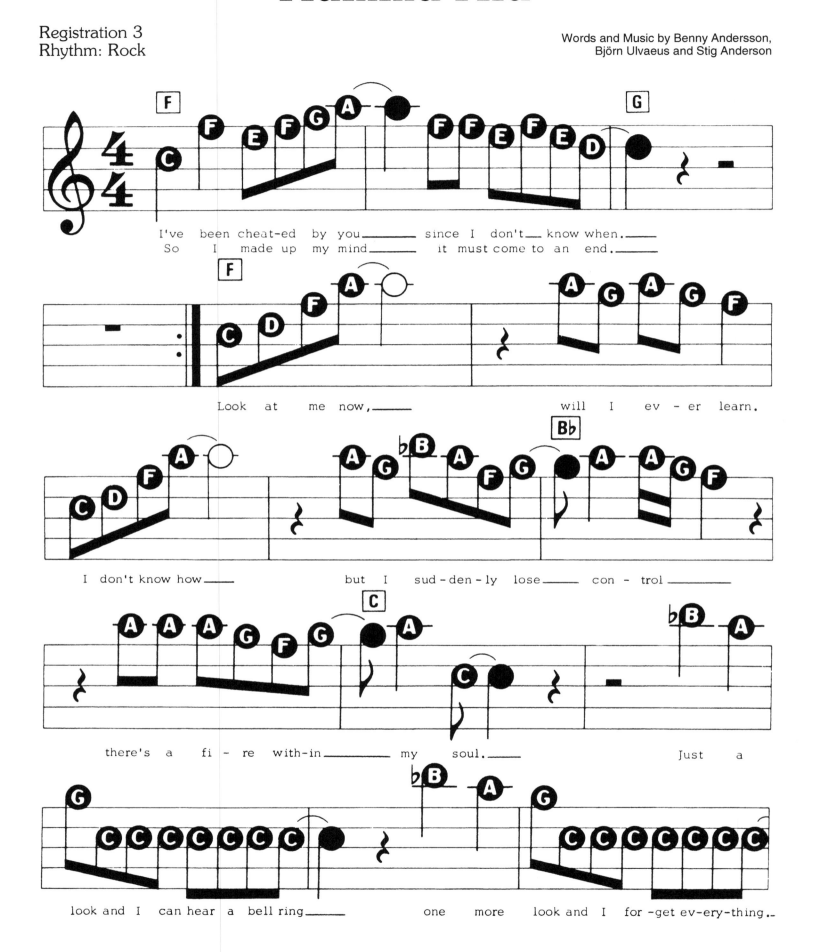

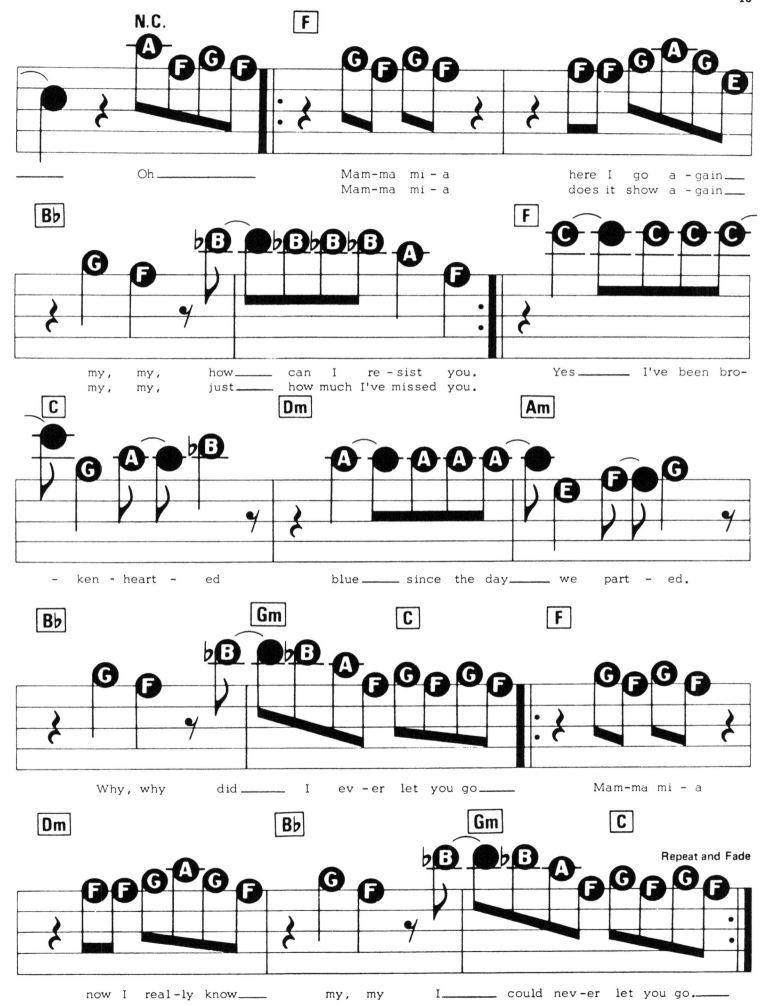

Oh _____ Mam-ma mi - a _____ here I go a - gain___
Mam-ma mi - a _____ does it show a - gain___

my, my, how_____ can I re - sist you. Yes_____ I've been bro-
my, my, just_____ how much I've missed you.

- ken - heart - ed blue_____ since the day_____ we part - ed.

Why, why did_____ I ev - er let you go_____ Mam-ma mi - a

now I real - ly know_____ my, my I_____ could nev - er let you go._____

Money, Money, Money

Registration 7
Rhythm: Rock

Words and Music by Benny Andersson
and Bjorn Ulvaeus

I work all night, I work all day to pay the bills I have to pay

ain't it sad And still there ne - ver seems to be a

sing - le pen - ny left for me that's too bad, In my dreams I

have a plan if I got me a wealt - hy man I

would-n't have to work at all. I'd fool a-round and have a ball.

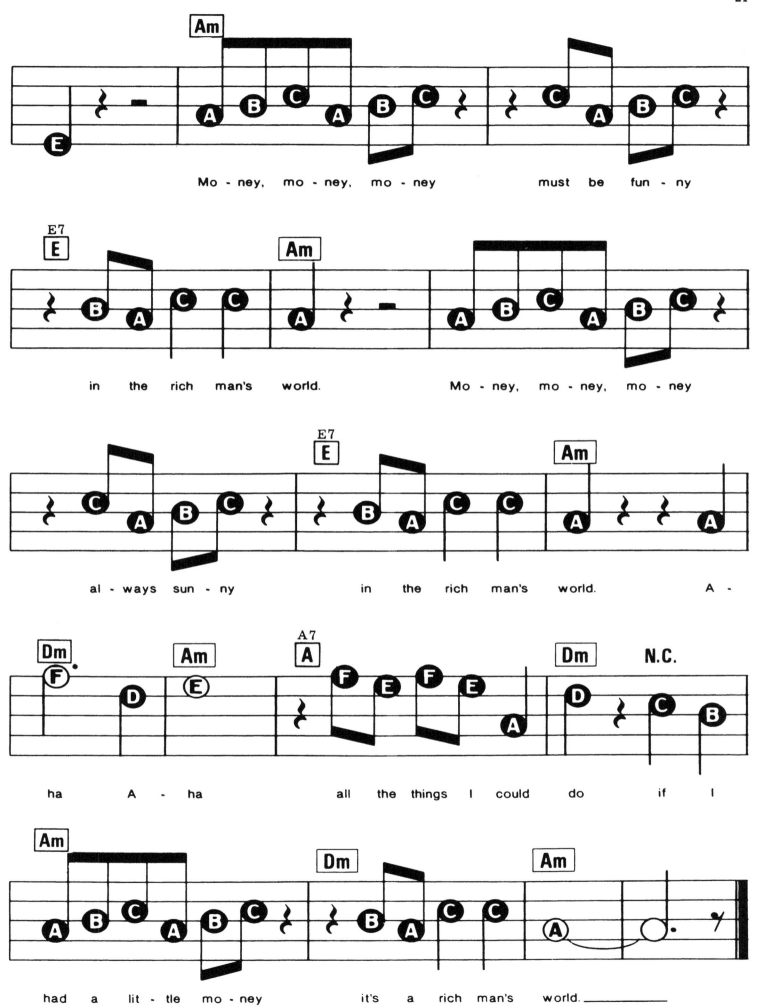

The Name of the Game

Registration 1
Rhythm: Rock

Words and Music by Benny Andersson,
Bjorn Ulvaeus and Stig Anderson

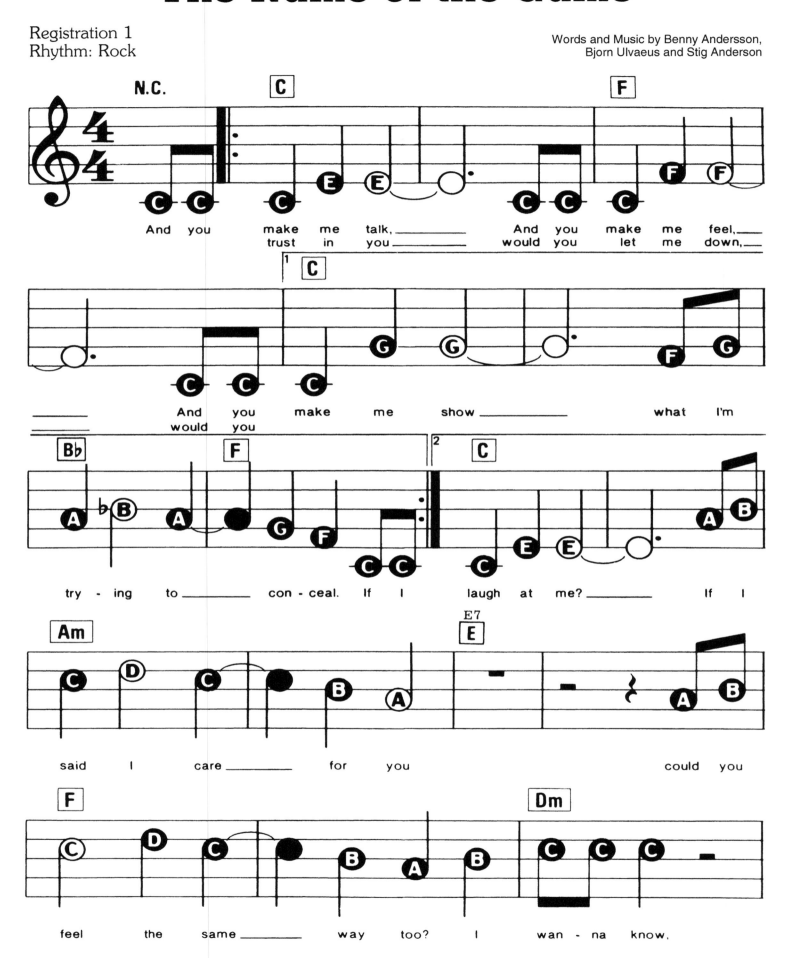

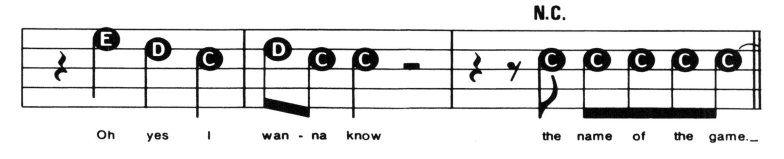

N.C.

Oh yes I wan - na know the name of the game._

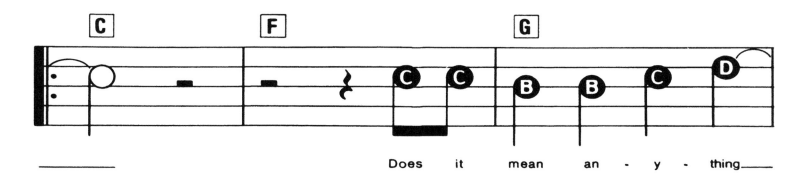

_____ Does it mean an - y - thing_____

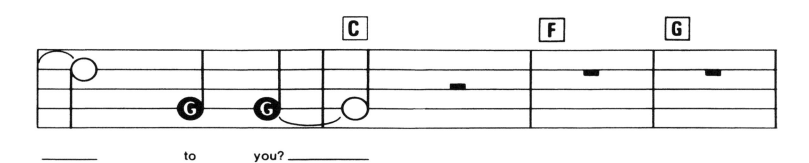

_____ to you? _____

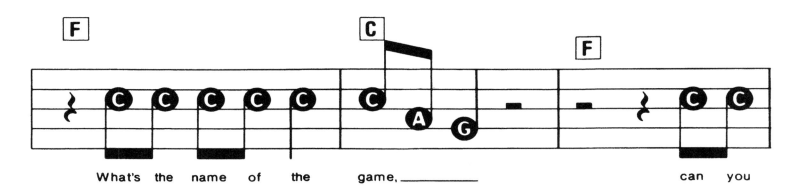

What's the name of the game, _____ can you

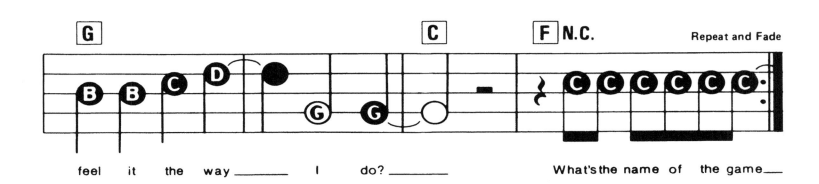

Repeat and Fade

feel it the way _____ I do? _____ What's the name of the game___

Our Last Summer

Registration 4
Rhythm: 8-Beat or Rock

Words and Music by Benny Andersson
and Bjorn Ulvaeus

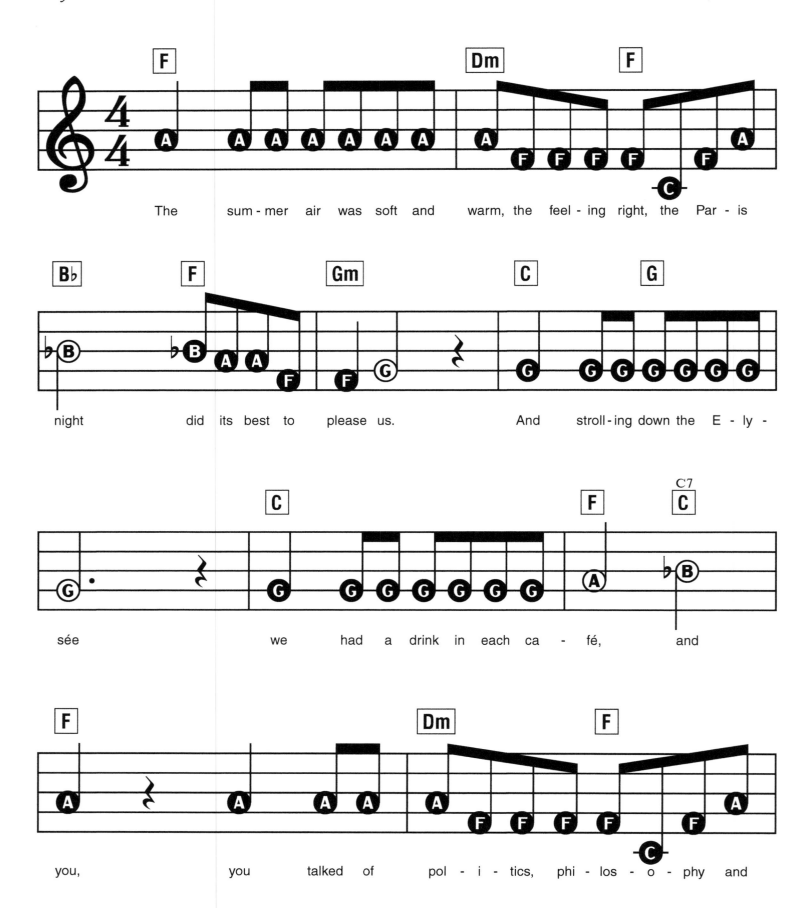

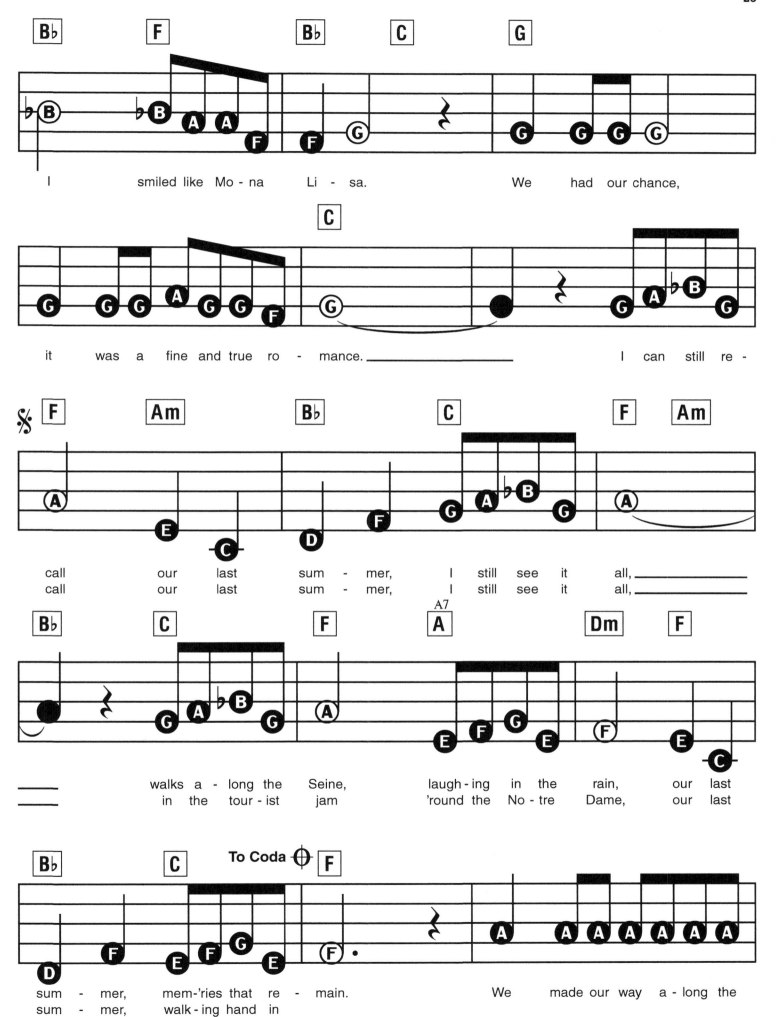

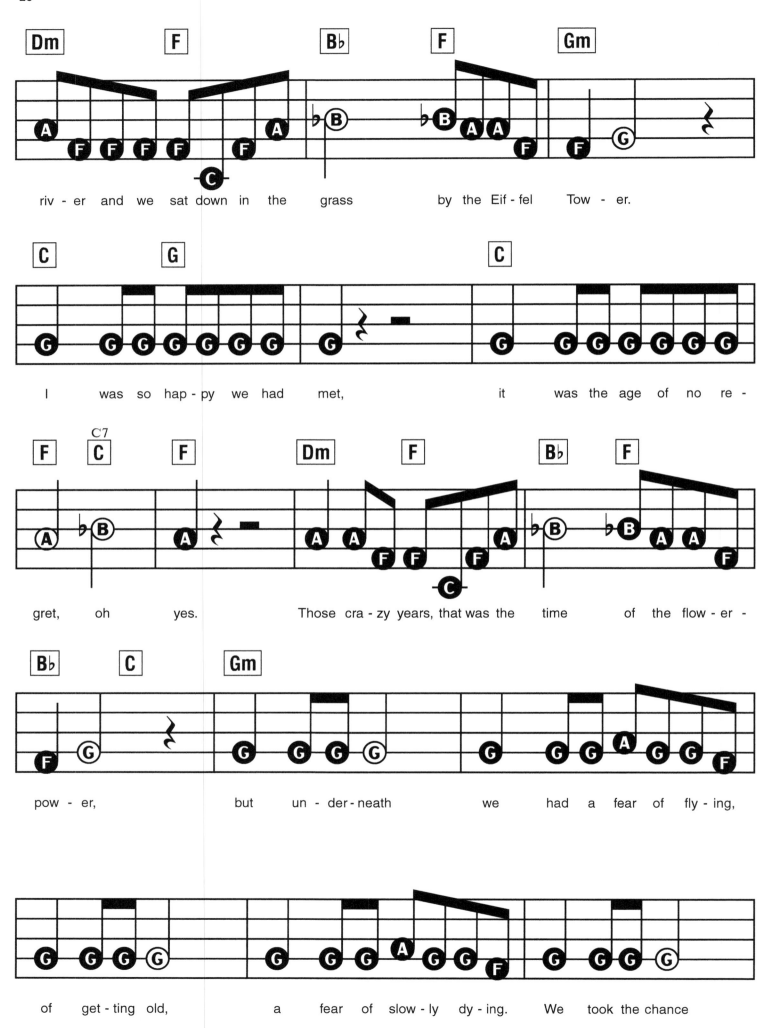

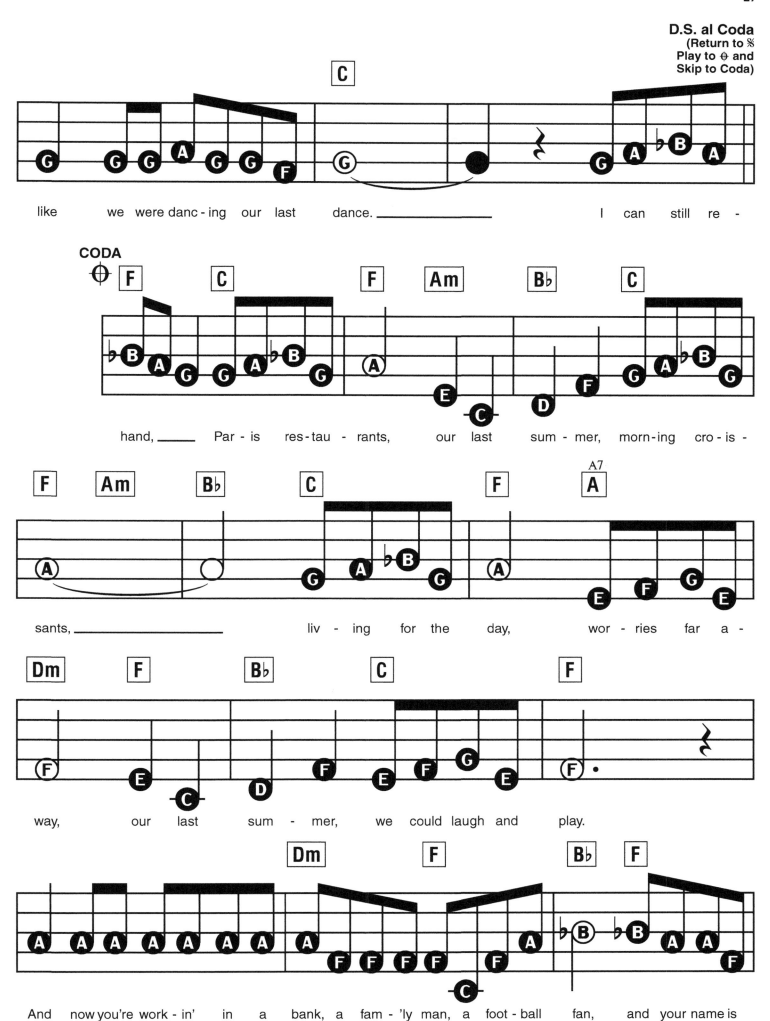

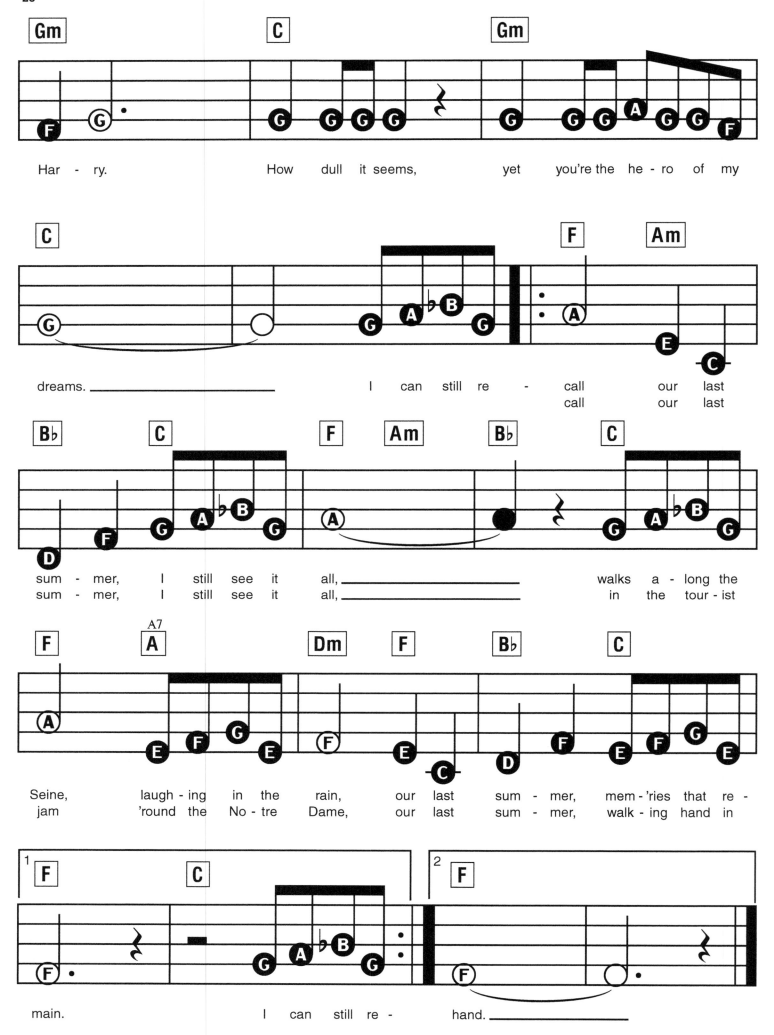

Super Trouper

Registration 1
Rhythm: Rock

Words and Music by Benny Andersson
and Bjorn Ulvaeus

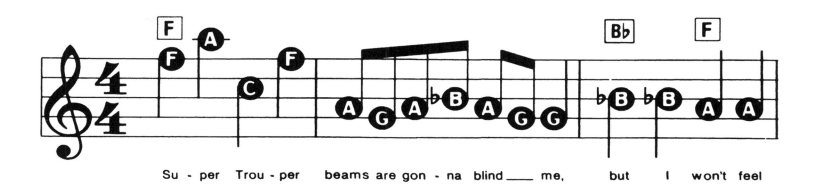

Su - per Trou - per beams are gon - na blind ____ me, but I won't feel

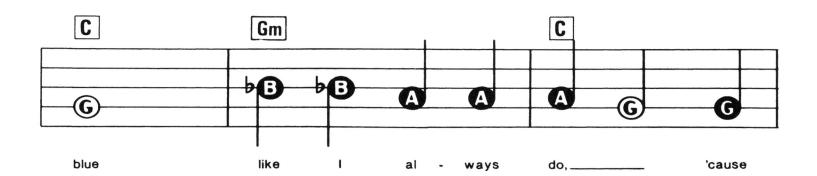

blue like I al - ways do, _____ 'cause

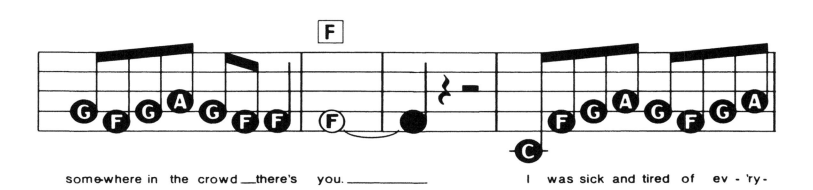

some-where in the crowd ___ there's you. _____ I was sick and tired of ev - 'ry-

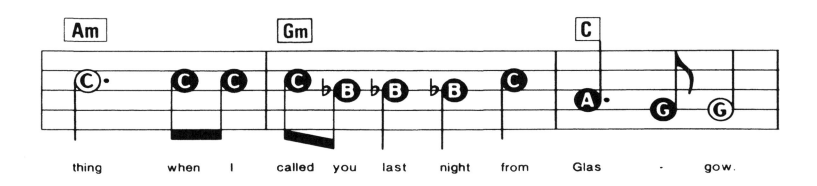

thing when I called you last night from Glas - gow.

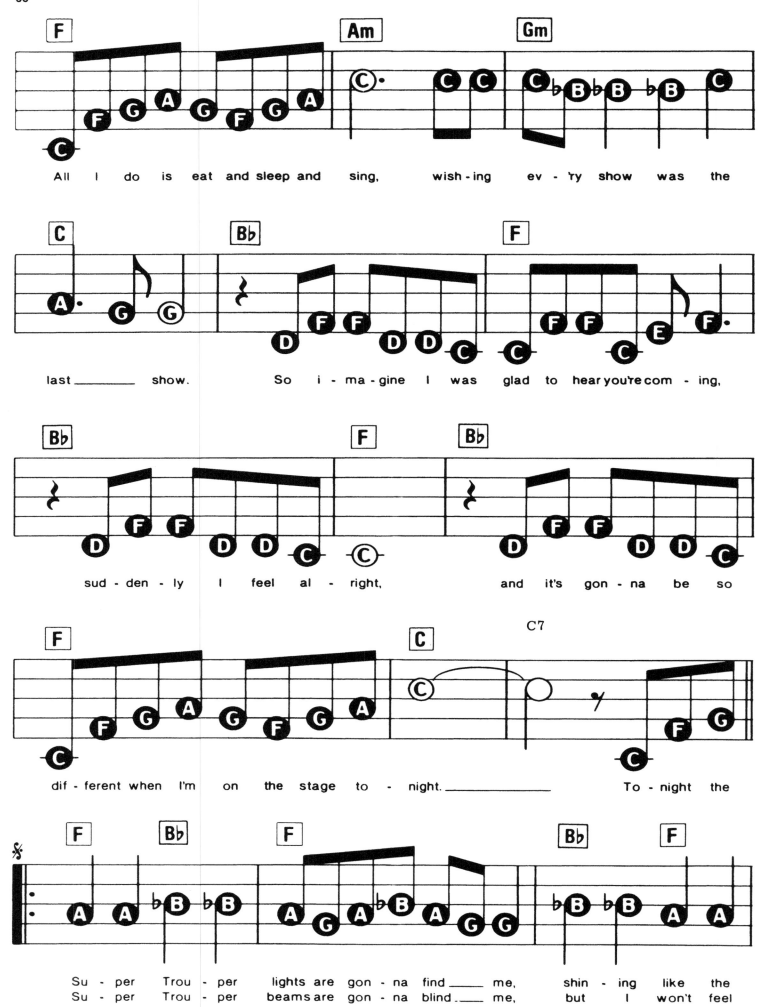

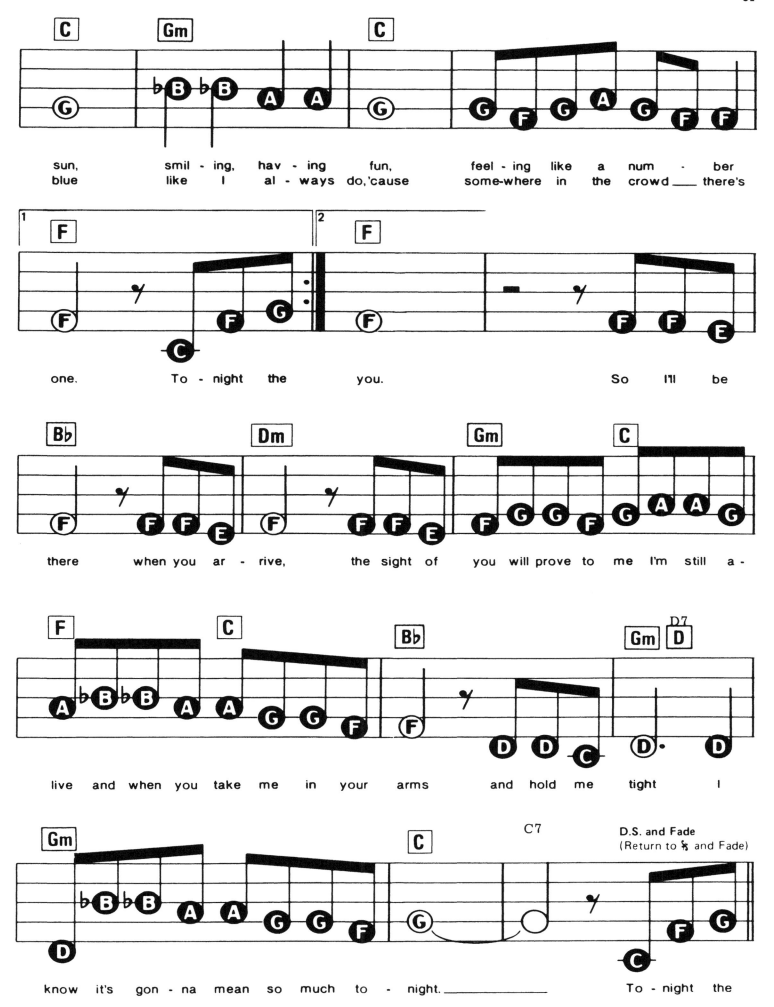

Slipping Through My Fingers

Registration 2
Rhythm: 8-Beat or Rock

Words and Music by Benny Andersson
and Bjorn Ulvaeus

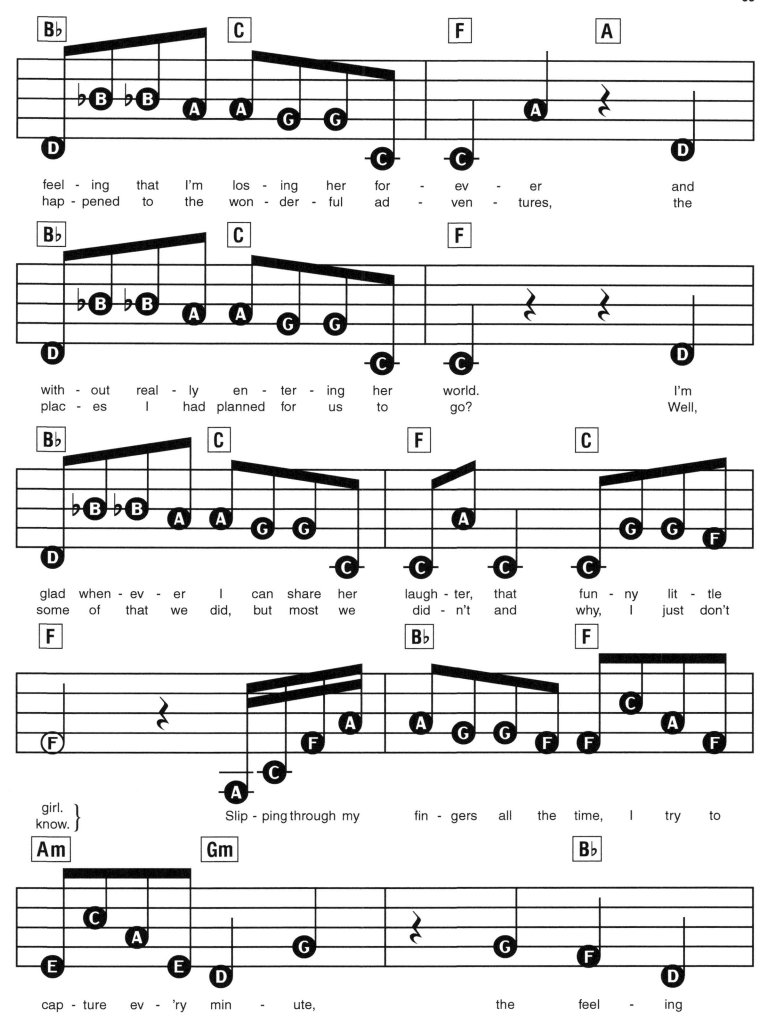

33

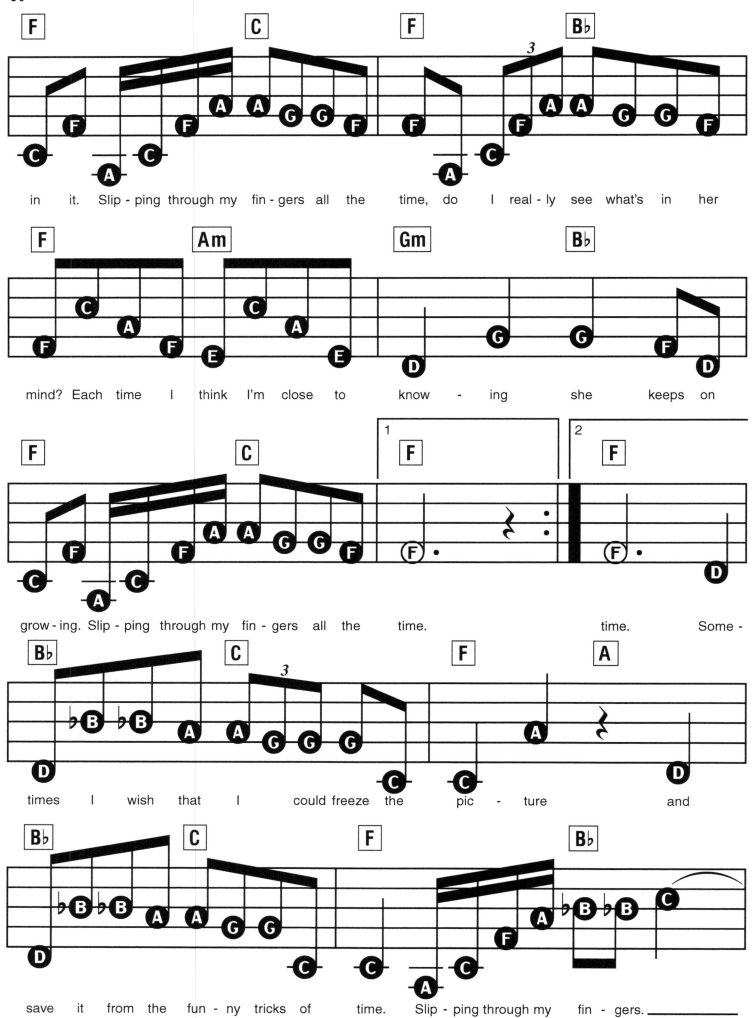

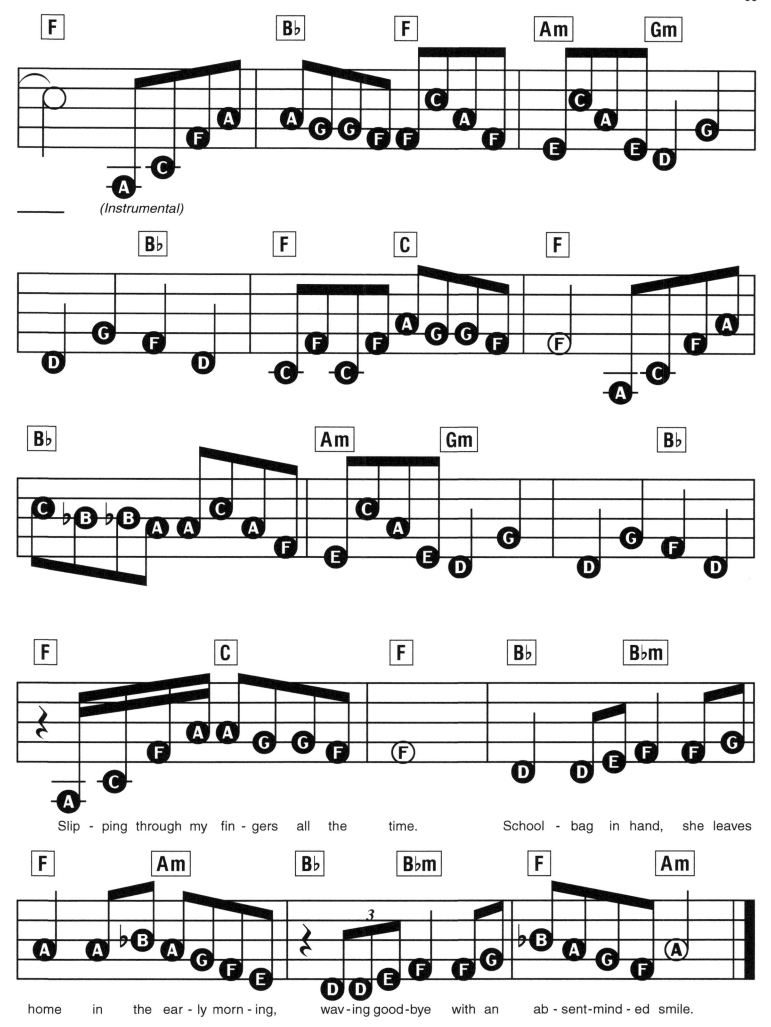

35

(Instrumental)

Slip - ping through my fin - gers all the time.   School - bag in hand, she leaves

home   in   the   ear - ly   morn - ing,   wav - ing good-bye   with an   ab - sent-mind - ed smile.

S.O.S.

Registration 1
Rhythm: Rock

Words and Music by Benny Andersson,
Bjorn Ulvaeus and Stig Anderson

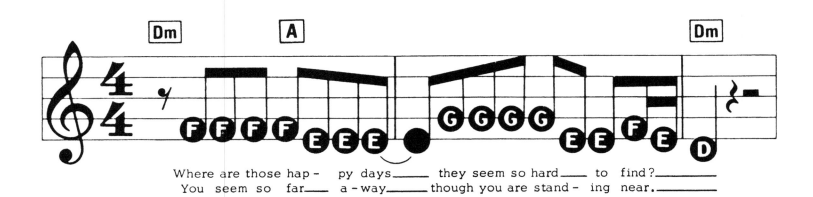

Where are those hap - py days___ they seem so hard___ to find?___
You seem so far___ a - way___ though you are stand - ing near.___

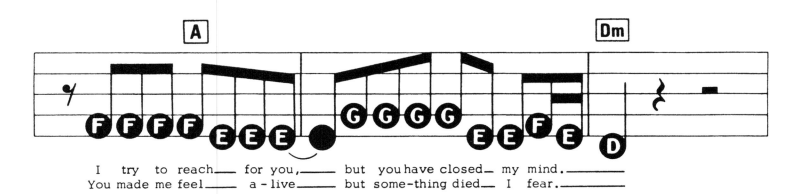

I try to reach___ for you,___ but you have closed___ my mind.___
You made me feel___ a - live___ but some-thing died___ I fear.___

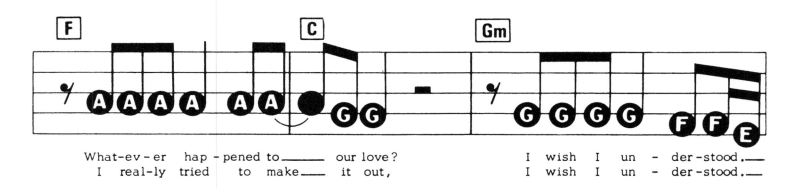

What-ev - er hap - pened to___ our love?   I wish I un - der-stood.___
I real-ly tried to make___ it out,   I wish I un - der-stood.___

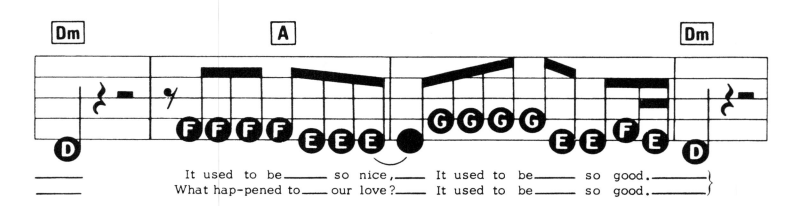

_____   It used to be___ so nice,___ It used to be___ so good.___
_____   What hap-pened to___ our love?___ It used to be___ so good.___

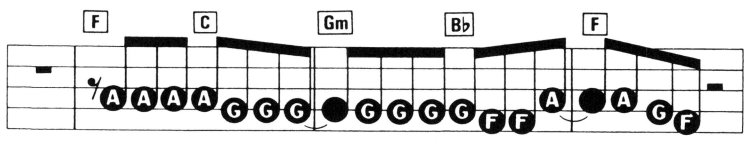

So when you're near_ me dar - ling can't you hear_ me S._ O. S._

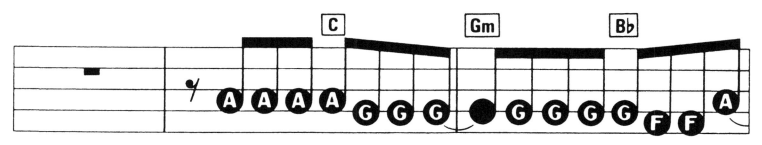

The love you gave_ me noth - ing else can save_ me S._

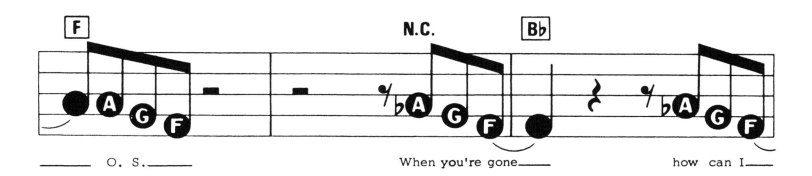

_ _ O. S._ When you're gone_ how can I_

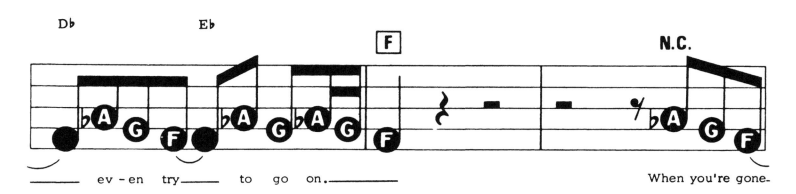

_ ev - en try_ to go on._ When you're gone_

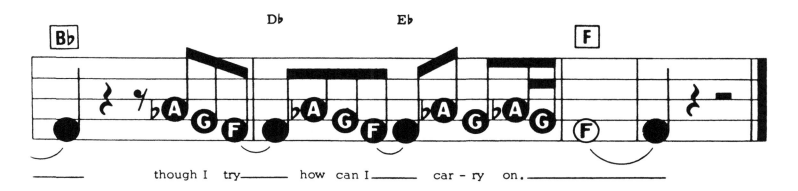

_ though I try_ how can I_ car - ry on._

Take a Chance on Me

Registration 1
Rhythm: Rock

Words and Music by Benny Andersson
and Bjorn Ulvaeus

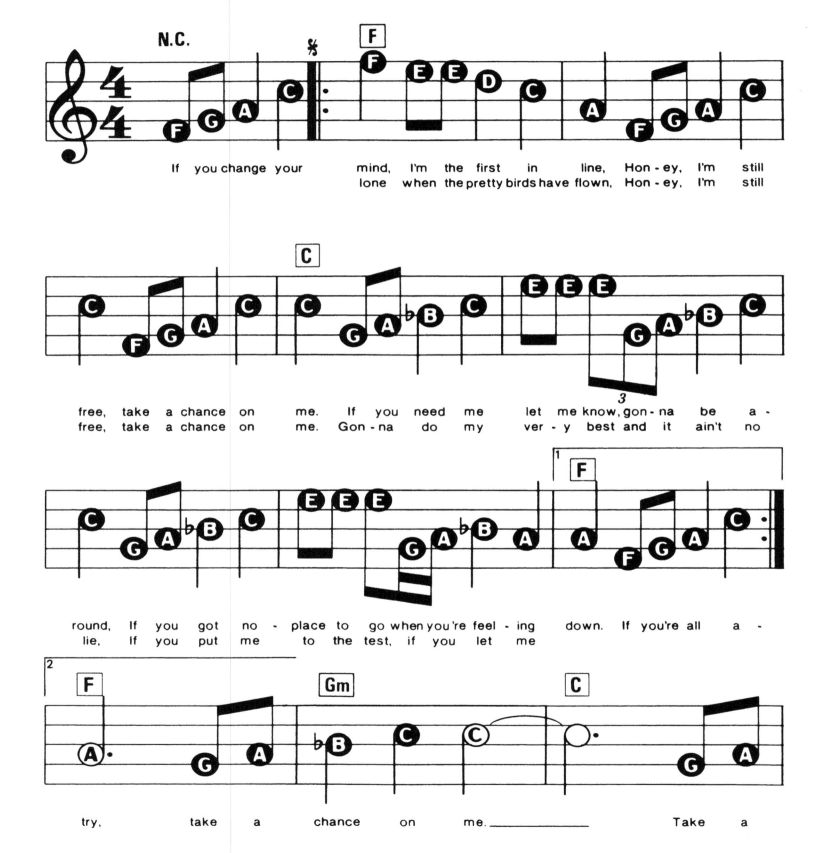

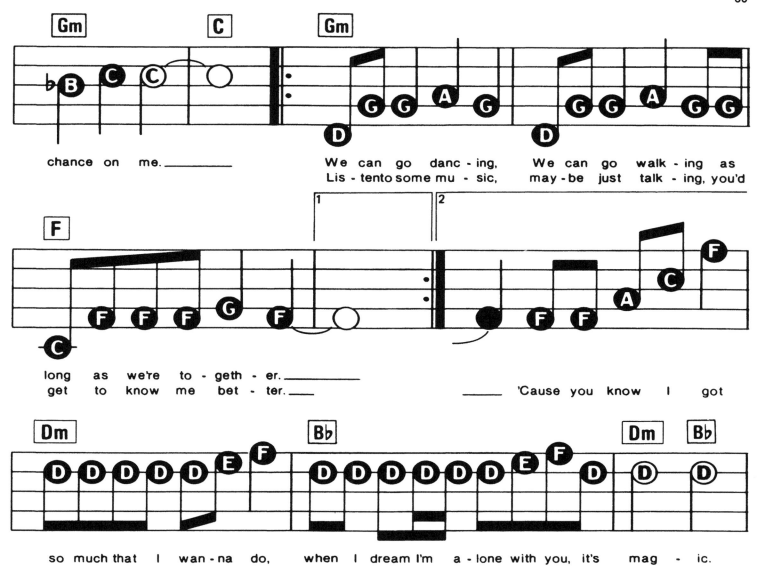

chance on me._____

We can go danc - ing,   We can go walk - ing as
Lis - ten to some mu - sic,   may - be just talk - ing, you'd

long   as   we're   to - geth - er._____
get   to   know   me   bet - ter.____   _____ 'Cause you know   I   got

so much that   I   wan - na   do,   when I dream I'm a - lone with you, it's   mag - ic.

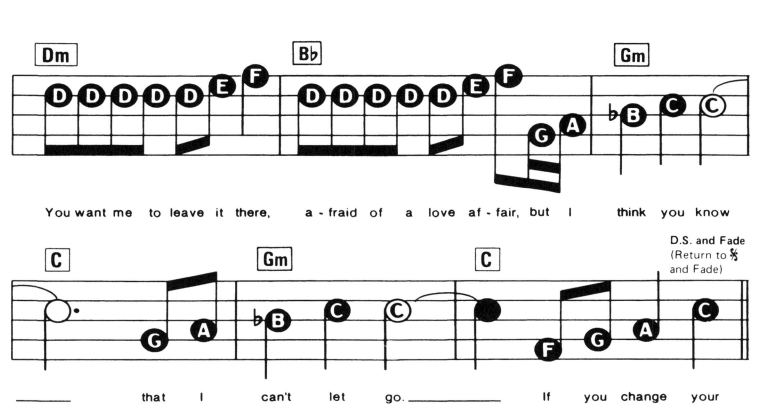

You want me   to leave it there,   a - fraid   of   a   love af - fair, but   I   think   you know

D.S. and Fade
(Return to 𝄋
and Fade)

_____   that   I   can't   let   go._____ If   you change   your

Voulez-Vous

Registration 3
Rhythm: Rock

Words and Music by Benny Andersson
and Bjorn Ulvaeus

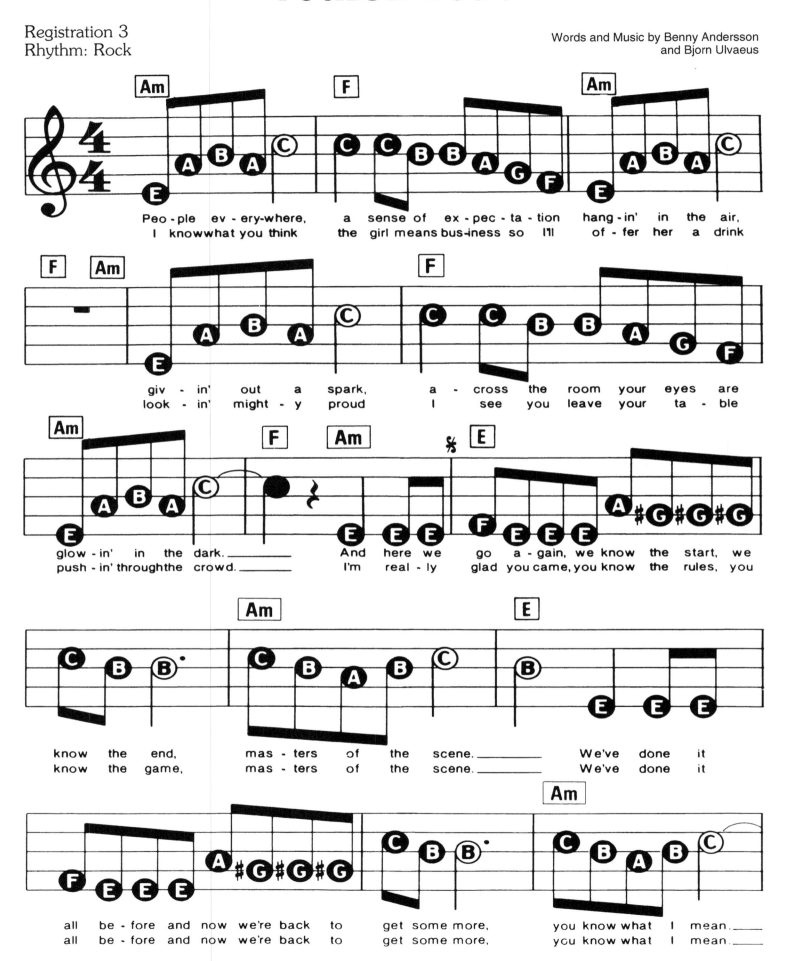

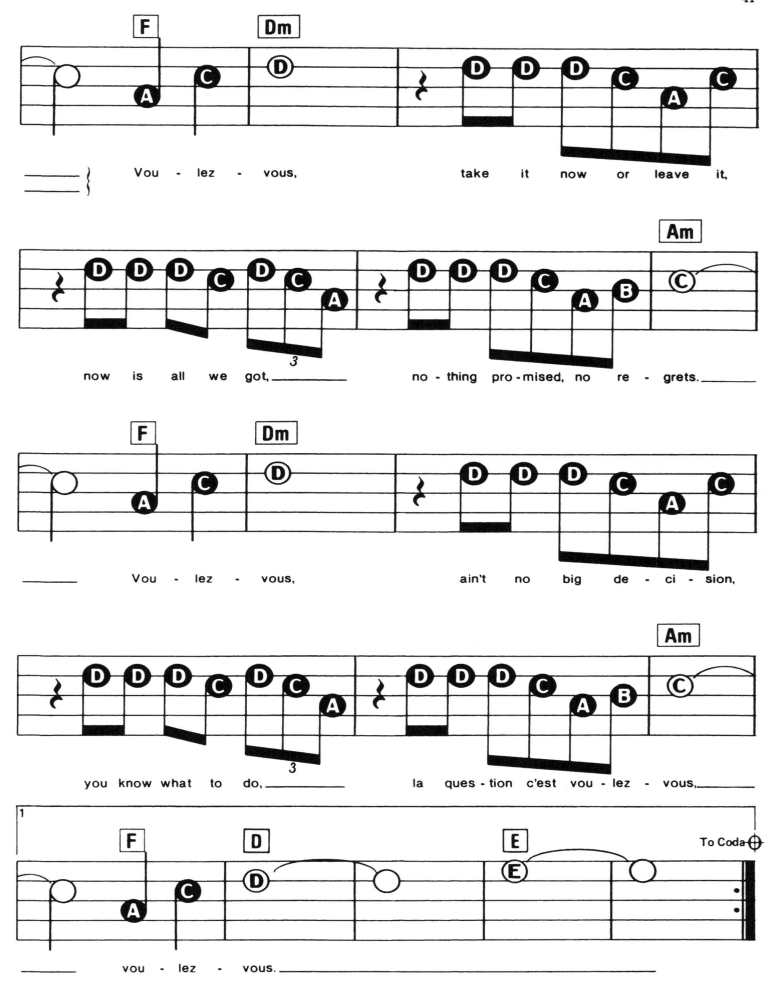

41

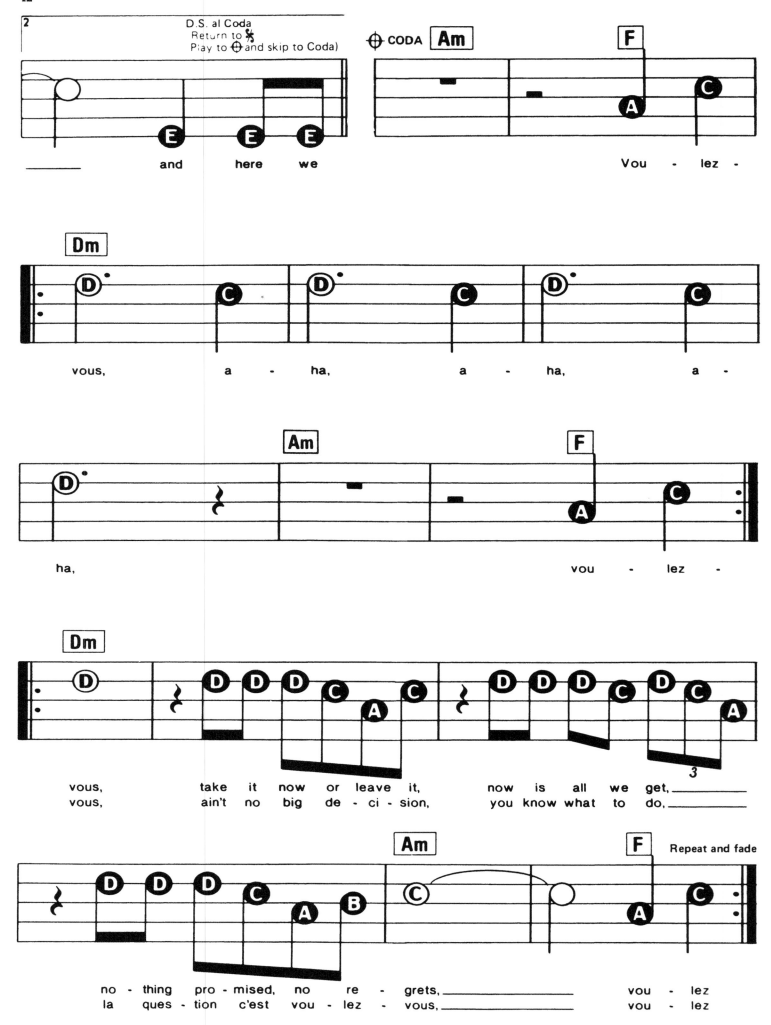

The Winner Takes It All

Registration 1
Rhythm: Rock

Words and Music by Benny Andersson
and Bjorn Ulvaeus

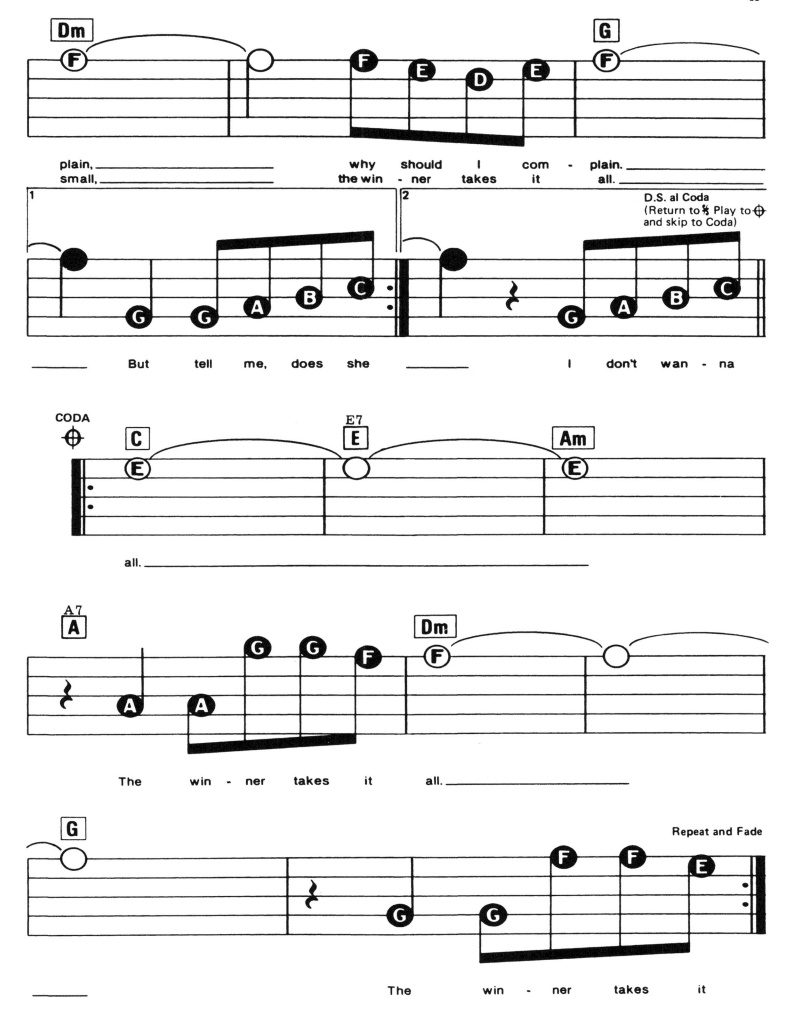

When All Is Said and Done

Registration 2
Rhythm: Folk or 8-Beat

Words and Music by Benny Andersson
and Bjorn Ulvaeus

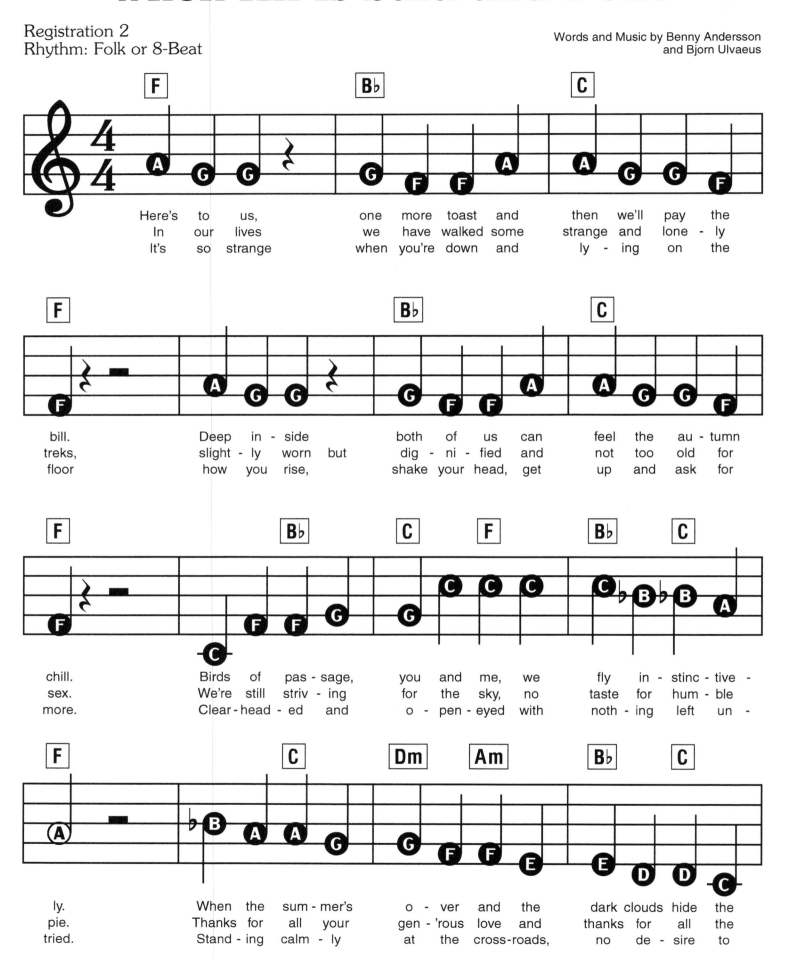

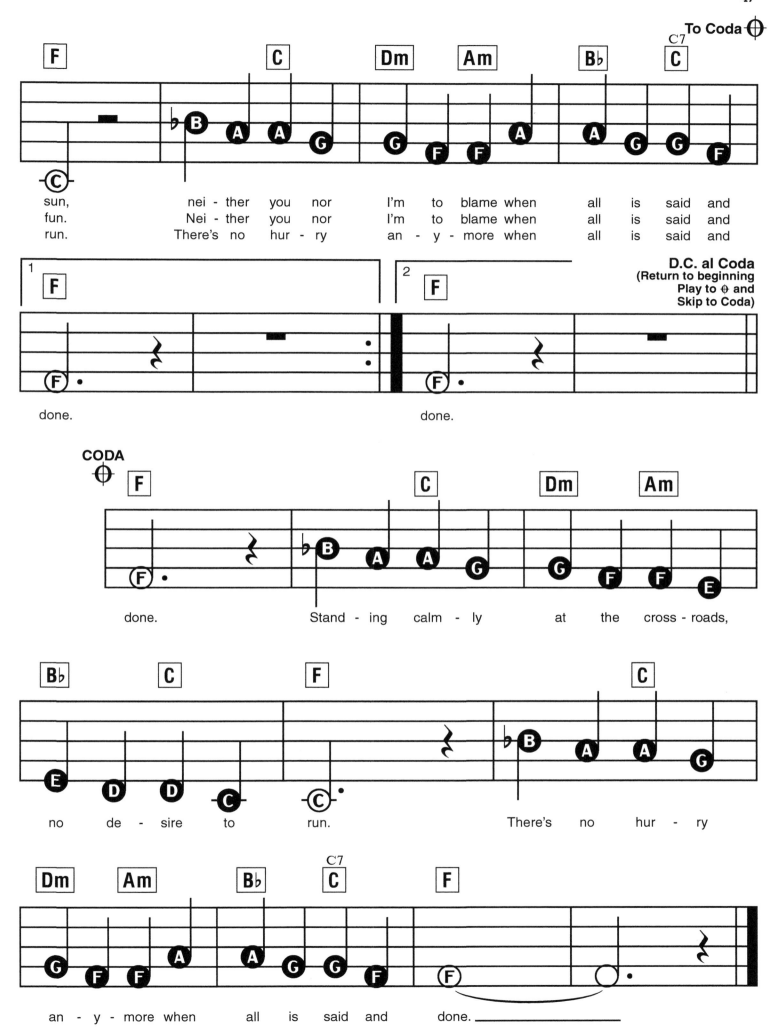

To Coda
D.C. al Coda
(Return to beginning
Play to ⊕ and
Skip to Coda)

sun,   nei - ther you nor I'm to blame when all is said and
fun.   Nei - ther you nor I'm to blame when all is said and
run.   There's no hur - ry an - y - more when all is said and

done.

done.

CODA

done.   Stand - ing calm - ly   at the cross - roads,

no de - sire to run.   There's no hur - ry

an - y - more when all is said and   done. _____

Registration Guide

- Match the Registration number on the song to the corresponding numbered category below. Select and activate an instrumental sound available on your instrument.

- Choose an automatic rhythm appropriate to the mood and style of the song. (Consult your Owner's Guide for proper operation of automatic rhythm features.)

- Adjust the tempo and volume controls to comfortable settings.

Registration

1	Mellow	Flutes, Clarinet, Oboe, Flugel Horn, Trombone, French Horn, Organ Flutes
2	Ensemble	Brass Section, Sax Section, Wind Ensemble, Full Organ, Theater Organ
3	Strings	Violin, Viola, Cello, Fiddle, String Ensemble, Pizzicato, Organ Strings
4	Guitars	Acoustic/Electric Guitars, Banjo, Mandolin, Dulcimer, Ukulele, Hawaiian Guitar
5	Mallets	Vibraphone, Marimba, Xylophone, Steel Drums, Bells, Celesta, Chimes
6	Liturgical	Pipe Organ, Hand Bells, Vocal Ensemble, Choir, Organ Flutes
7	Bright	Saxophones, Trumpet, Mute Trumpet, Synth Leads, Jazz/Gospel Organs
8	Piano	Piano, Electric Piano, Honky Tonk Piano, Harpsichord, Clavi
9	Novelty	Melodic Percussion, Wah Trumpet, Synth, Whistle, Kazoo, Perc. Organ
10	Bellows	Accordion, French Accordion, Mussette, Harmonica, Pump Organ, Bagpipes